Intermodal Transport
Containers
1980-1999

David G. Casdorph

Table of Contents

Field Notes
Sometimes photos weren't always possible, so hand-written notes were taken. A box like this will appear with relevant data, where appropriate.

ISSN 978-1-936829-41-5

Modern Transport History Press
Copyright © 2020 David G. Casdorph

Many thanks to Ed McCaslin for reviewing the manuscript, to John Becker for sharing some of his camera work for the chapter on CTI, and to Gary Walton for his support on this project.

ZIM Containers of the 1980s

The roots of ZIM go back to 1945 when the company was formed. The first ship was purchased in 1947. This ship, along with other ships acquired were converted to transport immigrants and supplies for the newly established state of Israel. ZIM expanded in the Fifties and Sixties with a focus on passenger ships. As air travel became more popular ZIM decided to discontinue passenger ship service and concentrate on cargo ships.

The Sixties initially brought in refrigerated ships and crude oil ships. In the Seventies, ZIM began to turn its focus on the emerging container industry, initially acquiring six special-purpose container ships. By 1972, ZIM boasted a container fleet of 5,500 TEU.

ZCSU 100495 is a Strick-built 40-foot standard-height container without vents (ISO 4300). These were marketed by Strick under the "Armorplate" line. The Strick Armorplate design includes heavy top and bottom rails, and one-piece sides with 19 reversed corrugations. The front wall Is also one-piece, but lacked the reverse corrugations. The doors have a large ZIM spread across the middle of both doors. In addition, a black צים is located in the upper left corner of the left door. Chassis is Theurer-built, Interpool owned, Zim operated ZINT 200535. Photographed in the City of Industry, California. December 30, 1985.

ZCSU 100846. Front panel of the Strick Armorplate showing ZIM logo in blue and black. Note the white background for the unit ID with a black inset border. The multi-colored label on the left is for an early form of automatic identification reader (KarTrak ACI used by railroads in the US). Port of Los Angeles. December 9, 1984

ZCSU 102894 on chassis ZCSZ 50151. Notice the small dash in the unit ID between the
owner code and unit number. Port of Los Angeles. December 9, 1984.

צים

In 1987, the Intermodal Transportation Association listed five owner codes for ZIM:

GSLU   ZIM Israel Navigation Co. Tel Aviv
ZBXU   ZIM Israel Navigation Company. New York/Haifa
ZCLU   ZIM Israel Navigation Co Ltd. Haifa
ZCSU   ZIM Container Service. Haifa/New York
ZIMU   ZIM Israel Navigation Company.

ZCSU 103967-1 on chassis ZCSZ 40047-7. This container was built in May 1973 by Strick.

ZCSU 104283 on chassis ZCSZ 60326 being transported by a Trailer Train BSF12 class 89'4" intermodal flat car passing through the City of Industry on 30 Dec. 1985. The black chalk box is to the right on both sides, while the ACI label is always to the rear on both sides.

ZCSU 105037 on chassis ZCSU 60187 gives a good layout of the markings in this broadside view. This container was built in August 1973 by Strick. The angled view of the other side of ZCSU 105037 is a poor quality image with color shifting due to incorrect use of an E-6 process 160T slide film.

ZCSU 203702. Now we jump up into the 200,000s as we see the entry of steel corrugated containers, still retaining the blue and black logos. This one is also vented (unlike those shown in the 100,000s). This design uses two logo panels with squared corrugations in a 2-44-2 arrangement. Vent casings are located at the top of each logo panel. Barely seen in this view is the huge "ZIM" spanning both doors. 40-foot standard height (ISO Type 4310).

ZCSU 207162 on a Strick built ZCSD 032518 chassis. Note the blue logo is always forward as seen here it is to the left of the lettering "Zim Container Service". 40-foot standard height (ISO Type 4310).

ZCSU 240635. In the late Eighties, ZIM standardized on brown for their dry box colors. The black ZIM was placed on the upper left door. Built by Hyosung. Note the American Bureau of Shipping (ABS) certification.

ZCSU 108192. The front wall had the large blue and black logo present.

ZCSU 202017-7 front wall.
It looks like markings for vertically placed container identification aren't so new.
No logos on the front wall on this gray corrugated steel paint scheme.

The logo on the sides of ZCSU 202017-7 is located near the top of the left logo panel with black ZIM CONTAINER SERVICE logo in the middle. The owner code, ZCSU was derived from the name, Zim Container Service. Note the vent casing is welded on and located between the two corrugations. The ten holes at at the bottom of the vent allow air to enter the interior. This photo also illustrates an example of the "peaked" logo panel.

ZCSU 202017-7 is shown on Strick-built, Interpool owned chassis ZCIP 01-150-2. Containers were still evolving during the 1970s and like most operators, ZIM acquired a variety of designs. This early 40-foot, vented, steel corrugated container has two logo panels each with peaked centers. Note the two large rectangular vents that span the top of each logo panel. There also appears to be a small narrow vent at the top center of the container (at least I can see what looks like holes on the bottom). My amateur photography skills trying for a tight crop cut off the right side of the photo a little more than desired.

ZIMU 203101-5. A poor quality photo, but the earliest 20-footer I could find in my collection. The ILX 2210 is the 70s era three letter country code and size-type code. The logo panels have a thick bead running vertically down the centers.

Zim Container Service Fleet Size						
Year	Type	Size	Quantity	TEU		Total TEU
1968-69	Not Listed					
1970-71	Listed - but no containers reported					
1972-73	Dry	20	5000	5000		5,500
	Insulated	40	200	400		
	Refrigerated	40	50	100		
1979	Dry	40	15000	30000		35,300
	Dry	20	5000	5000		
	Refrigerated	40	150	300		
1980	Dry	40	15000	30000		35,300
	Dry	20	5000	5000		
	Refrigerated	40	150	300		
1982	Dry	40	15000	30000		35,300
	Dry	20	5000	5000		
	Refrigerated	40	150	300		
1983	Dry	20	31000	31000		72,670
	Dry	40	18500	37000		
	Refrigerated	20	240	240		
	Refrigerated	40	840	1680		
	Specials	20	2050	2050		
	Specials	40	350	700		
1987	Dry	20	32000	32000		81,430
	Dry	40	21000	42000		
	Dry HC	40	1000	2000		
	Refrigerated	20	350	350		
	Refrigerated	40	1150	2300		
	Flat	20	520	520		
	Flat	40	90	180		
	Open-Top	20	900	900		
	Open-Top	40	390	780		
	Others	20	400	400		

Source: *Jane's Freight Containers* for the respective years list above.

ISO Size-Type Code 2040

Introduction

2040s (pronounced twenty-forties) are insulated (thermal) containers that have a 20-foot (actually 19'11") external length, an 8'0" outside height, and an 8'0" external width and have ports for the attachment of refrigeration/heating units. Most of the units depicted here are in the Australia to United States routes. These come from four major steamship lines:

• Associated Container Transportation (ACT logo, ACTU marks)
• Blue Star Line (BSL logo, BSLU marks)
• Hamburg Südamerikanische Dampfschifffahrts Gesellschaft (Columbus Line, Hamburg Süd logos, SUDU marks)
• Shipping Corporation of New Zealand (Shipping Corporation of New Zealand logo, NZCU, NZSU marks)

Most of the units built were steel-framed GRP/FRP (composite materials) designs. But, there were a number of traditional sheet-and-post designs, as well as the early specialized Graaff "Sandwich" composite types.

Associated Container Transportation (Australia) Ltd.

ACTU 700147. This is a steel-framed composite sided insulated container. There are three reinforcement strips on the sides. This is part of a mixed design series numbered ACTU 700000-703605. Photographed in March 1987 at the City of Industry, CA.

ACTU 702906. Built by Crane Fruehauf. This is a five panel sheet-and-post side design. Part of the mixed design series ACTU 700000-703605. Photographed in March 1987 at the City of Industry, CA.

ACTU 703189 has sheet-and-post sides with four full-width panels plus end panels. Part of the mixed design series ACTU 700000-703605. Photographed in August 1989 in the Port of LA/Long Beach, CA area.

ACTU 703773 is a five-panel sheet-and-post design. Part of the mixed design series ACTU 700000-703605. Photographed in November 1989 in the Port of LA/Long Beach, CA area.

ACTU 703915. Five-panel sheet-and-post sides. Part of the ACTU 703606-704260 series. This container appears to be second-hand as evidenced by the logo remains on the left side. The only readable part is "(????) Line Genoa".

ACTU 705328. Steel-framed GRP/FRP sides insulated container. This comes from the mixed design series ACTU 704261-709949. The GRP/FRP (Glass Reinforced Plastic/Fibreglass Reinforced Plywood) sides are made as fitted piece. Note the fasteners/rivets around the edges where the FRP sheet meets the frame.

ACTU 705387 from the same series as above. The fasteners/rivets form the same patterns as ACTU 705328. However, this one has three stiffeners on the side FRP sheet. I believe these stiffeners were added later in the container's service.

ACTU 705915 (above) and ACTU 706678 (below) were both built by Crane Fruehauf (United Kingdom). Sheet-and-post design. Both have the five panel sides. And both of these are from the mixed design series ACTU 704261-709949. Photographed in March 1987 (above) and December 1989 (below).

ACTU 707435. GRP/FRP type construction needed repairs too, as we can see with this interesting patch to the right of the ACT logo. Photographed in March 1987 in the City of Industry, CA.

ACTU 707876 features the red Australian National Line logo on its sides. The ANL container operations were eventually bought in 1998 by CMA CGM. This is a steel-framed GRP/FRP side insulated container. Again, this is from the mixed design series ACTU 704261-709949. Photographed in August 1989 in the Port of Long Beach/Port of LA area.

ACTU 708226 on chassis TPPZ 000110. Photographed October 11, 1989. A door fastener is seen at the bottom of the panel on the right just above the frame.

ACTU 710667 with ANL logo. The door fastener on this container is located higher in the panel. Photographed in March 1989 at the City of Industry Southern Pacific yards.

ACTU 710872 with the ANL logo. This is part of a one-thousand container series, ACTU 709950-710949. Photographed in November 1989. Port of LA/Long Beach, CA.

ACTU 711448 is a sheet-and-post design. Series, ACTU 710950-711647, totaling 698 units. The door fastener on this container is the more common simple hook on the lower rail centered above the chassis' tandem axles. October 1989.

ACTU 712143 was built by Inta-Eimar of Spain. This comes from the series, ACTU 711648-712449 with 802 units. Photographed in November 1989.

Detail of the Inta-Eimar builder's plate on ACTU 712143. The stamped construction number is 57548.

ACTU 712143 detail of the front wall showing a full width panel and a narrower panel to the left in this photo. Also, there are no "tunnels" on 2040s.

A small plate showing the right door shows the owner's name and address, manufacturer, timber treatment, and tare weight of the container. ACTU 712143.

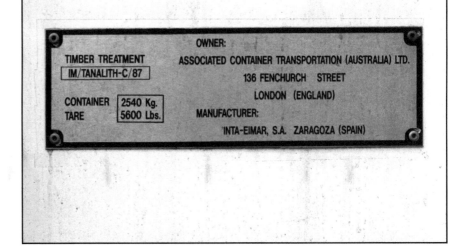

TIMBER TREATMENT	OWNER:
IM/TANALITH-C/87	ASSOCIATED CONTAINER TRANSPORTATION (AUSTRALIA) LTD.
	136 FENCHURCH STREET
CONTAINER 2540 Kg.	LONDON (ENGLAND)
TARE 5600 Lbs.	MANUFACTURER:
	INTA-EIMAR, S.A. ZARAGOZA (SPAIN)

ACTU 712143

BSLU 560592 with *Crusader Service* heraldry. FRP design container with three side stiffeners. Notice the external absence of fasteners/rivets along the frame where it meets with the side panel. Photographed in August 1989.

Field Notes
BSLU 561384. GBX 2040. Built 2-78 by Duramin. 929 cu.ft. Construction number T0284.

Left, BSLU 560605 same design as above, but without the three side stiffeners. This container was built in August 1977 by Duramin. The view shows the two portholes on the front wall to be used for adding refrigeration/heater devices. Photographed in April 1981.

New Zealand Line, Ltd

NZCU 200069. Steel-framed GRP/FRP insulated container on ICSZ 166047 leased to American President Lines. Photographed in December 1989 in the greater Port of LA/Port of Long Beach, CA area.

NZCU 210554. Steel-framed five panel sheet-and-post insulated container. Built by Crane Fruehauf in England. Photographed in December 1989 in the greater Port of LA/Port of Long Beach, CA area.

NZCU 210696. Steel-framed five panel sheet-and-post insulated container. Built by Crane Fruehauf in England. This one is on a Utility built INTZ 783026 being leased to SCNZ (Shipping Corporation of New Zealand. Photographed in the early 1980s.

NZCU 210696 showing the front wall with the two large "port-holes" for refrigeration/heater attachments.

NZCU 210709. Another steel-framed five panel sheet-and-post unit. Photographed in November 1989.

NZCU 210712. Built by Crane Fruehauf. Chassis is Fruehauf built NLSZ 20424. Photographed in the early 1980s.

NZCU 210712. View of the doors. Some reefer and insulated containers have some form of the huge door hinges shown here. Data shown on the right door:

MAX. G.W.	20320 kg
TARE	2168 kg
CU. CAP.	26.3 M³

NZCU 760426-4. Steel-framed GRP/FRP insulated container. Photographed in December 1989.

Field Notes
NZSU 761159.
Built 2-83 by Crane Fruehauf. Model KA12-20PA.
Construction No. FK-1108.
Order No. 0528.

The two photos below show details of the front wall and lower port-hole on NZSU 762045. This unit was built in 2-83 by Crane Fruehauf. Model KAZ-20-ST-119.

SUDU 202164 is a Graaff "sandwich" sides insulated container. This is similar to the GRP/FRP construction with a single sheet for the sides. This is a nine-grooved version with even spacing between the grooves. Photographed in November 1989.

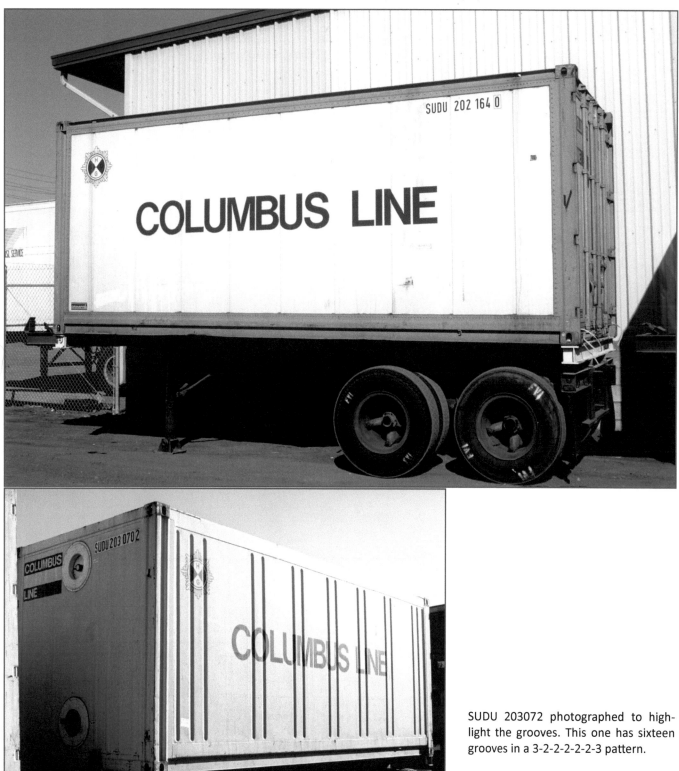

SUDU 203072 photographed to highlight the grooves. This one has sixteen grooves in a 3-2-2-2-2-2-3 pattern.

SUDU 203072, view of the doors. This one has four hinges per door. Data on the right reads, Max. Gross 52,910 lbs 24,000 kg, Tare 5,950 lbs 2,700 kg, Max. Payload 46,950 lbs 21,300 kg, Cube 950 cuft 27,0 m³. Photographed in October 1989.

SUDU 205271. Steel-framed with nine-groove sandwich sides. This is part of a series numbered SUDU 205000-205579 (580 containers) built by Graaff in March and April 1989.

SUDU 215904 is part of a huge series, SUDU 214000-215999 (2,000 units). This is a steel-framed GRP/FRP sided design. Maximum gross on these were the old standard for 20-foot containers of 20,320 kg (44,800 lbs). Tare is 2,300 kg (5,070 lbs). Photographed on October 11, 1989.

SUDU 216419 comes from a 1,000 strong series numbered SUDU 216000-216999. Maximum gross is 20,320 kg (44,800 lbs). Tare is 2,400 kg (5,290 lbs). Marking and lettering practices of these early containers have many differences from today's containers. This one has the weight and capacities data on the sides as well as the more well-known door position. The chassis is Flexi-Van owned TPPZ 000111-7 that weighs 6,460 lbs. Photographed on October 11, 1989.

SUDU 217304. Steel-framed GRP/FRP construction. This one comes from a series of
310 units numbered SUDU 217000-217309. Maximum gross is 20,320 kg (44,800 lbs).
Tare is 2,400 kg (5,290 lbs). Photographed on October 11, 1989.

SUDU 218716. Steel-framed GRP/
FRP design. Series is 218306-219335
(1,130 containers). These were built in
1979 by Industriewerke Transportsys-
teme in West Germany. Serial number
7909119-1895.

SUDU 221183, front, doors and roster views.

SUDU 221183 comes from the SUDU 221000-221801. These were built in July through September 1979 by Thyssen Industrie GmbH in West Germany. Construction No. 8471. Steel-framed GRP/FRP construction. Max. Gross 24,000 kg 52,910 lb. Tare 2,300 kg 5,070 lb. Max. Payload 21,700 kg 47,840 lb. Cube 26.5 m³ 936 cuft.

SUDU 221538 was built by Thyssen Uniformtechnik in 1979. Series, SUDU 221000-221801. Photographed on October 11, 1989.

SUDU 221645. Built in September 1979 by Thyssen Uniformtechnik. Construction No. 9018. Max. Gross 24,000 kg 52,910 lb. Tare 2,300 kg 5,070 lb. Max. Payload 21,700 kg 47,840 lb. Cube 26.5 m³ 936 cuft. Series, SUDU 221000-221801.

SUDU 223353. Steel-framed GRP/FRP design. Built by Graaff. Series, SUDU 223340-223399. Chassis, TPPZ 000154 with Uni-Flex logo. Photographed in September 1989 in the greater Port of LA/Port of Long Beach, CA area.

SUDU 224248. Steel-framed GRP/FRP design. Built by Graaff. Series, SUDU 224000-224424. Chassis, TPPZ 000139. Photographed in October 1989 in the greater Port of LA/Port of Long Beach, CA area. Max. Gross 44 800 lbs 20 320 kg. Tare 5 070 lbs 2 300 kg.

SUDU 226178 roster view. Built by Thyssen Uniformtechnik in November 1982. Contruction No. 13518A. Steel-framed GRP/FRP construction with three side stiffeners. Series, SUDU 226000-226649 (650 units). Photographed in September 1989.

SUDU 226178 quarter rear view. Maximum gross is 20,320 kg (44,800 lbs). Tare is 2,400 kg (5,290 lbs). Cube is 26,7 m³ (940 cu.ft.). Chassis is TPPZ 000111.

SUDU 227003. Built by Graaff. Steel-framed GRP/FRP design. Series, SUDU 227000-227499 (500 units). Chassis, TPPZ 000151. Photographed in September 1989.

Detail of logo in the upper corner on the front wall of SUDU 227003 and SUDU 229016.

SUDU 229016. Built by Graaff. Steel-framed GRP/FRP design. Series, SUDU 229000-229149 (150 units). Chassis, TPPZ 000136. Photographed in September 1989.

Roster of SUDU ISO size-type 2040 Containers 1989

Marks	Series		OL	OH	OW	Tare	Qty	Builder	Year
SUDU	201000	201129	19-10	8-0	8-0	5730	130	Graaff	1988
SUDU	201200	201499	19-10	8-0	8-0	5730	300	Graaff	
SUDU	202000	202179	19-10	8-0	8-0	5950	180	Graaff	
SUDU	203000	203119	19-10	8-0	8-0		120		
SUDU	203200	203399	19-10	8-0	8-0		200		
SUDU	204000	204119	19-10	8-0	8-0		120		
SUDU	205000	205579	19-10	8-0	8-0	5180	580	Graaff	1989
SUDU	210000	211279	19-10	8-0	8-0		1280		
SUDU	213000	213812	19-10	8-0	8-0		813		
SUDU	214000	215999	19-10	8-0	8-0	5070	2000		
SUDU	216000	216999	19-10	8-0	8-0	5290	1000		
SUDU	217000	217309	19-10	8-0	8-0	5070	310		
SUDU	217310	218014	19-10	8-0	8-0		705	Industriewerke	1979
SUDU	218015	218305	19-10	8-0	8-0		291		
SUDU	218306	219235	19-10	8-0	8-0	5070	930	Industriewerke	1979
SUDU	219236	219435	19-10	8-0	8-0		200	Industriewerke	1979
SUDU	220000	220499	19-10	8-0	8-0	5290	500	Concargo	1978
SUDU	220500	220699	19-10	8-0	8-0	5290	200	AHI	
SUDU	221000	221499	19-10	8-0	8-0	5070	500	Thyssen	1979
SUDU	221500	221801	19-10	8-0	8-0	5070	302	Thyssen	1979
SUDU	222437	222536	19-10	8-0	8-0		100		
SUDU	223000	223049	19-10	8-0	8-0		50		
SUDU	223150	223199	19-10	8-0	8-0		50		

Marks	Series		OL	OH	OW	Tare	Qty	Builder	Year
SUDU	223340	223399	19-10	8-0	8-0		60	Graaff	
SUDU	224000	224424	19-10	8-0	8-0	5070	425	Graaff	
SUDU	225000	225339	19-10	8-0	8-0		340		
SUDU	226000	226649	19-10	8-0	8-0	5290	650	Thyssen	1982
SUDU	227000	227499	19-10	8-0	8-0		500	Graaff	
SUDU	229000	229149	19-10	8-0	8-0		150	Graaff	

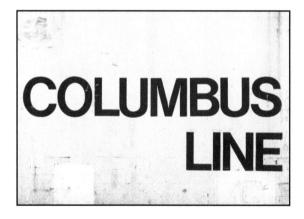

A selection of logos and lettering applied to the sides of SUDU insulated containers seen during the 1980s. The top two are corner logos. The remaining three photos show the large "billboard" style applied to the central area of the sides. The HSDG initials stand for Hamburg-Südamerikanische-Dampfschiff-fahrts-Gesellschaft.

COLUMBUS LINE

HAMBURG SÜD

Santa Fe's
1980s Containers

Not all of the containers operated by the Santa Fe in the 1980s were gleaming white 48-foot containers with big blue logos. In the mid-1980s Santa Fe began operating ISO 40-foot standard-height, ISO 40-foot high-cube, and ISO 45-foot high-cube containers from various container leasing companies and former steamship lines. Some even had plates attached for placement of the Santa Fe logo.

Later, steel corrugated 48-foot high-cube containers were introduced to the growing fleet. And finally, near the end of the decade, Santa Fe brought on a whole new fleet of 48-foot high-cube sheet-and-post containers.

SFTU 206201. A standard-height 40-foot steel-corrugated "van" container from Sea Containers. Many of the these steel-corrugated containers have a total of 48 corrugations with two logo panels per side. However, the arrangement of those corrugations often varied by customer or builder. Here we see a squared 6-38-4 configuration. Photographed in December 1989. VTTX 300491 was built in February 1963 and converted to COFC flat car in the mid-Eighties.

SFTU 206428. Another standard-height steel-corrugated 40-foot van container from Sea Containers. This one in a blue scheme acquired second-hand by Sea Containers. This container has a squared 2-44-2 corrugation configuration. Note the plastic 8-pin vent covers at the top of each logo panel. This comes from the mixed source series SFTU 206000-206800. The flat car, TTWX 971701 was built 9-73 by Bethlehem Steel. Trailer Train class BSH20A. Photographed in November 1988.

SFTU 206720 in Uni-Flex livery. Standard-height steel-corrugated 40-foot van container. Uni-Flex containers at the time of this photo was part Itel Containers International Corporation. Side corrugations are 2-44-2. Note the steel rectangular vent covers at the top of the logo panels. This is still a part of the SFTU 206000-206800 group. Photographed in December 1989.

SFTU 258172. Steel-corrugated 45-foot high-cube van container. Santa Fe operated a small number of units that are former Lykes Bros. Steamship containers. The Lykes' 45-foot containers a somewhat unique in both design and paint scheme. Side corrugations beveled 2-2-35-2-1 with the "filler" vent covers located in the space between the first and second corrugations in the 40-foot section of the container. It also has two fork lift pockets. The container in the lower position is GSTU 900276. The well car is DTTX 63305 built in April 1987 by Gunderson's Portland, OR plant. Photographed on April 25, 1987.

Santa Fe's Containers 1989

Marks	Number Range		OL	OH	OW	Notes
SFTU	205000	205081	40	8-6	8-0	1
SFTU	206000	206800	40	8-6	8-0	2
SFTU	258000	258185	45	9-6	8-0	3
SFTU	258200	258249	45	9-6	8-0	
SFTU	258255	258672	45	9-6	8-0	3
SFTU	259537		48	9-6		4
SFTU	259700	259799	48	9-7	8-6	
SFTU	259999		48	9-6	8-6	5

Marks	Number Range		OL	OH	OW	Notes
SFTU	296000	296098	40	9-6	8-0	6
SFTU	689000	689299	48	9-6	8-6	7
SFTU	689300	689599	48	9-6	8-6	8
SFTU	689600	689624	48	9-6	8-6	
SFTU	689525	689675	48	9-6	8-6	9
SFTU	689700	689899	48	9-6	8-6	10
SFTU	759701	759781	48	9-7	8-6	11
SFTU	768000	768999	45	9-6	8-6	12

Notes

1. Steel-corrugated Triton observed. 205010 (3-84 Tokyu Car 2390 cuft ex-TRIU 407540), 205011 (Jindo 2392 cuft), 205029 (4-87 Hyundai 2387 cuft), 205031 (Tokyu Car 2390 cuft), 205061 (11-86 Jindo 2382 cuft ex-TRIU 471342), 205070 (5-87 Hyundai 2387 cuft)

2. Mixed design and mixed source series. Steel-corrugated Sea Containers, Uni-Flex and Itel observed. 206148 (Sea Containers), 206172 (Santa Fe circle-and-cross logo on attached metal plate), 206197 (Sea Containers), 206201 (Sea Containers), 206250 (Santa Fe circle-and-cross logo on attached metal plate), 206408 (Sea Containers), 206427 (Sea Containers), 206428 (Sea Containers), 206468 (Santa Fe circle-and-cross logo on attached metal plate), 206470 (Sea Containers), 206540 (Santa Fe circle-and-cross logo on attached metal plate), 206720 (Uni-Flex), 206763 (Itel).

3. Former LYKU or identical specifications. Steel-Corrugated.

4. Sea Containers observed. Steel-Corrugated.

5. Xtra logos and trim. 259999 built by Miller.

6. Itel observed. 296038. Steel-Corrugated.

7. Delivered new to Santa Fe. Sheet and post. Monon. 3473 cuft. 9,959 lbs tare.

8. Delivered new to Santa Fe. Sheet and post. Monon. 3434 cuft. 9,710 lbs tare.

9. Steel-corrugated Sea Containers observed. 689658 (1986 HMIC 9,830 tare 3457 cuft)

10. Single white 48 on red panel. Monon. 3473 cuft. 10,700 lbs tare (687787), 9,959 (689887).

11. Xtra logos and trim. 759780.

12. Delivered new to Santa Fe. Insulated. Monon. 3219 cuft. 9,556 lbs.

SFTU 258476. Former LYKU (Lykes) unit. 45-foot high-cube steel corrugated container. The flat car is SFLC 901314 built in 11-78. Photographed on November 15, 1986 passing through San Bernardino, CA.

SFTU 259537 is a 48-foot high-cube steel corrugated van container. Though it takes a second look, this container does have two logo panels, in this case peaked panels. Side corrugations beveled 3-3-34-3-3. The chassis is Flexi-Van FSFL 4080155 with a red labeled "Return to Santa Fe Ramp Hobart". Photographed on July 11, 1987.

SFTU 689142 (top) and SFTU 689403 (lower) are both 48-foot sheet-and-post containers built by Monon, but from two different orders. The different positions of the container numbers are a quick distinguishing feature of these two early series. The numbers are SFTU 689000-689299 and SFTU 689300-689599 (300 each). The car is SFLC 254200, unit D. This is the lead car in the Santa Fe class DS-8 built at Gunderson's Portland, Oregon plant in 1989.

SFTU 689203 (top position) is a 48-foot high-cube sheet-and-post container. Gross weight 67,200 lbs. Tare weight 9,320 lbs. In the lower position is BNAU 281342. Burlington Northern was getting into the act of acquiring 48-foot containers at about the same time. The well car is SFLC 254230, unit C. Photographed in December 1989.

SFTU 689220 (top position) is a sheet-and-post 48-foot high-cube van container built by Monon. These were coming on stream circa 1988-89. The container in the lower position is HDMU 407373 from a series of one-thousand containers numbered HDMU 406818-407817. The well car is DTTX 63305, unit E, a Trailer Train set with full Santa Fe Econo-Stack marks. Photographed in January 1989.

SFTU 689445 (top) and 689102 (lower) on SFLC 254200 again, this time unit B. This photo was taken in August 1989, the same month as the build date on the well car. San Bernardino, CA.

SFTU 689787 is a 48'L x 9'6"H x 102"W sheet-and-post van container built by Monon. Gross weight, 67,200 lbs. Tare weight, 10,700 lbs. Series, SFTU 689700-689899. Bottom container is BNAU 280823 from the BNAU 280500-281499 series. The double-stack well car is SFLC 254230, unit D. Photographed in December 1989.

SFTU 759780 (top position). This 48-foot high-cube sheet-and-post van container comes from the series, SFTU 759701-759801. Obviously, this one is in full XTRA regalia. Below is SFTU 206281, another standard-height 40-foot steel-corrugated van container. Side corrugations beveled 2-35-2. This particular container is an ISO 4300, and has no vents. The double-stack well car is SFLC 254125 (unit B) built under Thrall Job 474 in March 1988.

SFTU 768461 is a 45-foot high-cube insulated container built by Monon. Gross weight 67,200 lbs. Tare 9,556 lbs. Cube 3,219 cubic feet. Monon built a thousand of these for Santa Fe. Series, SFTU 768000-768999.

SFTU 768709. Insulated 48-foot high-cube container seen at Santa Fe's Hobart Yard in January 1989. The insulated containers didn't stay on Santa Fe's container roster for very long, they started disappearing in late 1989.

SFTU 768980 (top position). comes from the SFTU 768000-768999 series. Below it is SFTU 206763, in Itel Containers International orange (though almost red, compare to well car). Side corrugations, squared 2-44-2 with plastic three-pin vent covers in the space between the first and second corrugation from each corner. Double-stack well car SFLC 254116 was built in March 1988 by Thrall Car. Light weight of the whole quintuple set is 190,200 lbs. Photographed in January 1989.

Han Jin Container Lines
The Beginnings

Originally branded as Han Jin Container Lines (and hence HJCL logos) was more well known as Hanjin Shipping Co. Ltd. It was created in South Korea in 1977.

By 1989, Han Jin had registered a modest fleet of 5,000 containers — all 40-foot standard-height types. A few years later, by 1987, Han Jin's fleet had grown to just under 18,000 containers, still all 40-footers, but now including both standard-heights and high-cubes.

Finally, by 1989, the fleet had upped its num-

bers to just over 35,000 units and now including 40-foot high-cube refrigerated containers and 20-footer dry van containers as well. By this time, Han Jin had acquired Korea Shipping Corporation (branded KS Line).

The 35,000 units included a small quantity of KS Line containers in the total. But, apparently it took Han Jin several years to round up and register the remaining KS Line units.

HJCU 690141 is a 40-foot high-cube refrigerated container built by Nippon Fruehauf. Note the 32,500 kg maximum gross weight, an early beginning for what would become standard for most 40-foot containers in the future. ABS certified (American Bureau of Shipping). Owner is Mitsubishi International Corporation.

HJCU 700753. Standard-height 40-foot dry van container. Built 1-21-1979 by Hyundai. Model HD-1AA-250. Construction № 400754. The vent casing on this one spans the top of each logo panel. The front wall has nine corrugations and the ABS seal on the first corrugation from the left. Photographed in January 1981.

HJCU 701484. Standard-height 40-foot dry van. Side corrugations squared 2-42-2. The vent casings on this one are medium-sized rectangular located in the top center of each logo panel. Note the front ISO corner posts are grooved. Chassis is Bertolini built HJCZ 32667. Photographed on May 24, 1986.

HJCU 701768. Built on 3-16-79 by Hyundai. Model HD-1AA-250. Construction № 401769. Standard-height 40-foot dry van container. Vent casings span the top of each logo panel. Side corrugations-squared 2-42-2. Front ISO corner posts grooved. Chassis is Trailmobile-built HJCZ 32070. Photographed in May 1981.

HJCU 702191. Standard-height 40-foot dry van container. Vent casings span the top of each logo panel. Side corrugationssquared 2-42-2. Front ISO corner posts grooved. Chassis is a Nautilus-owned, NLSZ 40016 leased to Hanjin.

HJCU 702344. Built on 5-12-79 by Hyundai. Model HD-1AA-250. Construction Nº 402345. Standard-height 40-foot dry van container. Vent casings span the top of each logo panel. Side corrugationssquared 2-42-2. Front ISO corner posts are grooved. Chassis Trailmobile-built HJCZ 30097. Photographed in May 1981.

HJCU 702674. Standard-height 40-foot dry van container. Vent casings span the top of each logo panel. Side corrugationssquared 2-42-2. The front ISO corner posts on this one are grooveless. Chassis HJCZ 2336. Photographed in May 24, 1986.

HJCU 702789. Standard-height 40-foot dry van container. Series HJCU 70000-702899. The lower rail is stepped on this design. Vent casings span the top of each logo panel. Side corrugations-squared 2-42-2. Flat car SLFC 902550. Photographed on May 24, 1986 on Cajon Pass in California.

HJCU 703169 front wall showing the nine corrugations. There are three corrugated panels depicted, the outer two with four corrugations each and the center panel with one corrugation. A relatively uncommon location for the American Bureau of Shipping seal that is located on the upper part of the first corrugation from left. Front ISO corner posts are grooved. Chassis is KCSZ 440655. Photographed November 11, 1986.

HJCU 703460. Standard-height 40-foot dry van container. Series 702900-703699 (800 units). Vent casings span the top of each logo panel. Side corrugationssquared 2-42-2. Front ISO corner posts are grooved. Photographed on May 24, 1986.

HJCU 704759. Standard-height 40-foot dry van container. Series 704001-704900 (900 units). Vent casings centered at the top of each logo panel. Side corrugationssquared 2-44-2. Front ISO corner posts are solid.

I want to point out an interesting point on the side's construction. There are twelve formed panels on this side. Going from left to right, the first panel is the one with a flat logo section and two corrugations on either side (2-L-2). The next five panels have 5 corrugations each, then one 2 corrugation panel, then three panels of 4 corrugations, followed by one panel of 1 corrugation and lastly the 2-L-2 logo panel on the right. Photographed on May 24, 1986.

HJCU 704925. Standard-height 40-foot dry van container. Series 704901-705100 (200 units). Vent casings span the top of each logo panel. Side corrugationssquared 2-42-2. Front ISO corner posts are grooved. Chassis Trailmobile-built HJCZ 30121.

HJCU 704925. Standard-height 40-foot dry van container. Series 704901-705100 (200 units). Vent casings span the top of each logo panel. Side corrugationssquared 2-42-2. Front ISO corner posts are grooved. Chassis Trailmobile-built HJCZ 30121. Photographed on May 24, 1996.

HJCU 705696. Standard-height 40-foot dry van container. Series 705601-705700 (100 units). Vent casings are large-sized and centered at the top of each logo panel. Side corrugationssquared 2-44-2. Front ISO corner posts are grooveless. Front wall has eight corrugations. Chassis is a Flexi-Van owned HJCZ 46512 leased to Hanjin. Photographed on January 25, 1986.

HJCU 705738. Standard-height 40-foot dry van container. Series 705701-705800 (100 units). Vent casings are large-sized and centered at the top of each logo panel. Side corrugationssquared 2-44-2. Front ISO corner posts are grooveless. Front wall has nine corrugations. Photographed on May 24, 1986.

HJCU 705866. Standard-height 40-foot dry van container. Series 705801-706100 (300 units). Vent casings are large-sized and centered at the top of each logo panel. Side corrugationsbeveled 2-35-2. Front ISO corner posts are grooveless. Photographed on May 24, 1986.

HJCU 706748. Standard-height 40-foot dry van container. Series 706701-707000 (300 units). Vent casings are large-sized and centered at the top of each logo panel. Side corrugationssquared 2-44-2. Front ISO corner posts are grooveless. Front wall has nine corrugations. Tare is 3,840 kg or 8,470 lbs. Chassis is a Flexi-Van owned UFCC 73096 leased to Hanjin. Photographed on May 24, 1986.

HJCU 707284. Standard-height 40-foot dry van container. Series 707001-707300 (300 units). Vent casings are large-sized and centered at the top of each logo panel. Side corrugationssquared 2-44-2. Front ISO corner posts are solid. Front wall has nine corrugations. Chassis is a Trailmobile-built HJCZ 32032.

HJCU 707753. Standard-height 40-foot dry van container. Series 707301-708300 (1,000 units). Vent casings are large-sized and centered at the top of each logo panel. Side corrugations-squared 2-44-2. Front ISO corner posts are grooveless. Front wall has nine corrugations. Chassis is HJCZ 32032.

HJCU 707827 and 707999. Both are standard-height 40-foot dry van container. Series 707301-708300 (1,000 units). Vent casings are large-sized and centered at the top of each logo panel. Side corrugationssquared 2-44-2. Front ISO corner posts are grooveless. Front wall has nine corrugations.

The flat car is SFLC 901287. The car was originally built for the New Orleans Public Belt in January 1979 by Bethlehem Steel Car.

HJCU 707867. Standard-height 40-foot dry van container. Series 707301-708300 (1,000 units). Vent casings are large-sized and centered at the top of each logo panel. Side corrugationssquared 2-44-2. Front ISO corner posts are grooveless. Front wall has nine corrugations. Chassis is HJCZ 89526. Photographed on October 3, 1985.

HJCU 708121. This container and those shown previously are shown in the "HJCL" paint scheme. Standard-height 40-foot dry van container. Series 707301-708300 (1,000 units). Vent casings are large-sized and centered at the top of each logo panel. Side corrugationssquared 2-44-2. Front ISO corner posts are grooveless. Front wall has nine corrugations. Chassis HJCU 32015.

HJCU 708395. Introducing the "Hanjin" logo paint scheme. In addition to a billboard size logo on the sides, the standard height is recognized in a small yellow box near the bottom under the container's number. All it shows is 2.6 on the top of label and 8 1/2 at the bottom of the label. Standard-height 40-foot dry van container. Series 708301-708800 (500 units). Vent casings are the eight-pin plastic removable design and centered at the top of each logo panel. Side corrugationssquared 2-44-2. Front ISO corner posts are solid. Front wall has eight corrugations. Photographed on May 24, 1986.

To the left is HJCU 708427. Also in the "Hanjin" paint scheme. Standard-height 40-foot dry van container. Series 708301-708800 (500 units). Vent casings are the eight-pin plastic removable design and centered at the top of each logo panel. Side corrugationssquared 2-44-2. Front ISO corner posts are grooveless. Front wall has eight corrugations. The container on the right is 713313. The flat car is ATSF 295187. Photographed on May 24, 1986.

HJCU 708843. "HJCL" paint scheme. This series (HJCU 708801-709300) was probably already in production when the "Hanjin" paint scheme was adopted. Standard-height 40-foot dry van container. Vent casings are large-sized and centered at the top of each logo panel. Side corrugationssquared 2-44-2. Front ISO corner posts are solid. Front wall has nine corrugations. Photographed on May 24, 1986.

HJCU 710414. A straight-on view showing the eight square corrugation front wall. Note the Korean Register label in between the first and second corrugation from the left, near the top. The series is HJCU 709301-711800 (2,500 units). This container was built in May 1986 by Hyundai. Model HD-1AA-256. HDHJ86-404913. Photographed on October 11, 1986 and already has a paint patch on this five month old container. Port of Los Angeles, California.

HJCU 710451. Series 709301-711800 (2,500 units).

HJCU 711043. Standard-height 40-foot dry van container. Vent casings are the eight-pin plastic removable design and centered at the top of each logo panel. Side corrugationssquared 2-44-2. Front ISO corner posts are solid. Front wall has eight corrugations. Photographed on May 24, 1986.

HJCU 711764. Front quarter-side view (above) and rear quarter view (left). Standard-height 40-foot dry van container. Series 709301-711800 (2,500 units). Vent casings are the eight-pin plastic removable design and centered at the top of each logo panel. Side corrugations squared 2-44-2. Front ISO corner posts are solid. Front wall has eight corrugations. Photographed on May 24, 1986.

HJCU 712259. One of the largest series of containers for Hanjin is HJCU 711801-715300 (3,500 units). Standard-height 40-foot dry van container. Vent casings are the eight-pin plastic removable design and centered at the top of each logo panel. Side corrugationssquared 2-44-2. Front ISO corner posts are solid. Front wall has eight corrugations. Photographed on May 24, 1986.

HJCU 713216 is seen riding on an ACF-built 89'4" flat car over Cajon Pass, CA. Standard-height 40-foot dry van container. Vent casings are the eight-pin plastic removable design and centered at the top of each logo panel. Side corrugationssquared 2-44-2. Front ISO corner posts are solid. Front wall has eight corrugations. Photographed on May 24, 1986.

HJCU 713701 on a Strick-built HJCZ 200023 chassis. Flat car is TTX 476431. Photographed on May 24, 1986.

HJCU 713708 detail views. On the left is a close-up of the Han Jin Container Lines Lettering with the space between the Han and Jin. Also in this view is the ownership notice, in this case it says "This Container is Owned By Saehan Merchant Banking Corporation 70, Sogong-Dong, Jung-Ku, Seoul, Korea and Korea Industrial Leasing Co., Ltd. 1 Sogong-Dong, Jung-Ku, Seoul, Korea". On the right side is a detail of the lower left door hinge and the ISO corner casting.

HJCU 713708. View of doors and lettering. Note the door bars are also the body color. In the upper left corner is the seal of the Korea Register. Below that is the label that reads, "Operator Han Jin Container Lines Ltd. Seoul Korea. On the left is a Customs Approval and CSC Safety metal plate. The upper right-hand side includes the container's identification, country code and ISO size-type code. On the bottom right is the builder's logo, this one built by Hyosung.

HJCU 717517 from the series HJCU 715801-717800 (2,000 units). Standard-height 40-foot dry van container. Vent casings are the narrow three-pin plastic removable design and located between the first and second corrugation from each end. Side corrugations-squared 2-44-2. Front ISO corner posts are solid. Front wall has eight corrugations. Photographed in December 1989.

HJCU 719602 from the series HJCU 717801-721600 (3,800 units). This container was built in August 1988 by Hyundai. Type HD-IAA-256R1. Manufacturer's № HDHJ88-410002. Standard-height 40-foot dry van container. Vent casings are the narrow three-pin plastic removable design and located between the first and second corrugation from each end. Side corrugations squared 2-44-2. Front ISO corner posts are solid. Front wall has eight corrugations. Photographed in December 1989.

HJCU 719602 straight on view on the doors. Flat, non-corrugated doors. "OTI" door handle arrangement. The weights and dimensions data shows are as follows: Max Gross 30,480 kgs/67,200 lbs. Tare Weight 3,860 kgs/8,510 lbs. May Payload 26,620 kgs/58,690 lbs. Cubic Capacity 67.⁵ m³/2384 Ft² (note unusual superscript for the decimal number in the m³ capacity). Chassis KCSZ 440117-A. Photographed in December 1989 in the Port of Los Angeles.

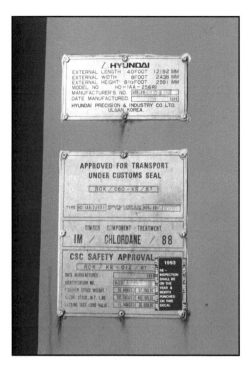

HJCU 719602 (left) Builders and CSC Approval plates. (Right) Detail of door hinge design. Photographed in December 1989.

HJCU 770353 is part of the series HJCU 770001-770500. This is a high-cube 40-foot container. Vents are located at the top of each logo panel. Side corrugations squared 2-44-2 in panels arranged as 2L1-5-5-5-5-2-5-5-5-5-1L2 (totaling eleven panels per side). Photographed on December 18, 1985.

HJCU 770590. Series 770501-772500 (2,000 units). Side corrugations, squared 2-44-2. Vent casings are the eight-pin replaceable plastic design and located at the top of each logo panel. In the bottom position is KSCU 415054 that has been re-branded with the Hanjin logo. Photographed on October 11, 1989.

HJCU 770865 view of the right side passing through Cajon Pass. Flat is a Trailer Train class ASH10A built by ACF in January 1974.

HJCU 770865 view of the right side and confirming the flat doors with "OTI" handles. This container comes from the HJCU 770501-772500. High-cube 40-foot dry van container.

HJCU 771516. This container comes from the HJCU 770501-772500. High-cube 40-foot dry van container. Rear roster view. The flat car is TTWX 980033 built by Bethlehem Steel in November 1978. Photographed in Cajon Pass on May 26, 1986.

HJCU 771516.
Front roster
view.

HJCU 771822 traveling on one of Trailer Train's venerable class F85C cars through Cajon Pass in California on a sunny May 24, 1986.

HJCU 772017 on SFLC 901515 just past Summit in Cajon Pass, California. Date, May 26, 1986.

The other half of SFLC 901515 with HJCU 772137. The flat car was built in December 1978 by Bethlehem Steel. May 26, 1986.

HJCU 772178. Tare weight is 4,080 kg or 9,000 lbs. The flat car is a rarely seen intermodal version of Trailer Train's F89A (most of these were former auto racks).

HJCU 772231 on Interpool owned chassis HJCZ 176707 on TTX 156039 (car built in September 1968 by Bethlehem Steel). Trailer Train class BSF11. May 26, 1986.

HJCU 772234. Sometimes containers coming off the production line when weighed edge just over the line to another base weight. In this case the container's weight is based firstly on the kilogram weight. Most of the containers in this series rounded out to 4,080 kg. However, this one rounded out to 4,050 kg or 8,929 lbs. Other containers at this weight include HJCU 771913 and HJCU 772168.

HJCU 772399 (top) and 708810 (bottom) in the "A" well of DTTX 72062 (Trinity Industries 2-89 built, class RWG52).

HJCU 776358. Suddenly lots of color on the front wall. In addition to the Hanjin logo and unit ID, there is now a yellow and black "Warning High Trailer", a mirrored red and white "Warning High Trailer" on the driver's side, and a yellow and black "2.9 High" label. August 1989.

HJCU 776358, roster view. High-cube 40-foot dry van container. Only three months old here, it was built in May 1989 by Hyundai. Type HDHJ89-710858. HD-HA-256R1 (the "R1" indicates a re-order). Series HJCU 775801-776800 . August 1989.

HJCU 776513. A changeover to the now standard narrow three-pin plastic removable vents marks a running production change in the series HJCU 775801-776800. December 1989.

Hanjin was a little late in the game to bring on 20-foot containers into the fleet. Here we see HJCU 850613, a standard-height 20-foot dry van container. Side corrugation configuration is 2-17-2 (21 corrugations total). Panels are 2L1-4-4-3-4-1L2, in six panels.

KSCU 211230. Standard-height 20-foot dry van container. 2-17-2 squared corrugations. Vents are centered in each logo panel near the top. This container has interesting door designs. The top and bottom recessed grooves are narrow. In the middle are two tall recessed lettering panels. May 24, 1986.

KSCU 213062. Standard-height 20-foot dry van container. 2-14-2 beveled corrugations. Vents are the three-pin plastic type and located between the first and second
corrugation from each end. Photographed on December 5, 1985 at the SP City of
Industry Yard.

KSCU 213305 is from the series, KSCU
213000-214399 (1,400 containers). Photographed on June 22, 1986.

KSCU 215547 is from the series KSCU 215000-216699 (1,700 containers). This one has had the KS Line logo painted out and replaced by the Hanjin logo.

KSCU 215547. Even the front wall gets the "circle-H" logo. This container has 2-17-2 square corrugated sides. This photo and the one previous was photographed in September 1989.

KSCU 411959-A. The old system of check digits used a letter to denote the "10" calculation, now replaced by the zero. This direct view of the front wall illustrates the use of eight square corrugations as part of its design.

KSCU 412100. Standard-height 40-foot dry van. This is a 39 bevel corrugated side container with two logo panels. Configuration is 1-37-1. The flat car is ATSF 294005. Photographed on March 27, 1986.

KSCU 412474 is also a 39 bevel corrugated side container. Series is KSCU 412000-412699 (700 containers). These have only a single vent per side, located to the right and placed in between the second and third corrugation to the left of the logo panel. Note the flat (non-corrugated) roof. Photographed on July 26, 1986.

KSCU 413362 is a 40 bevel corrugated side container, with corrugations arranged as 2-36-2. Again, there is only a single vent per side located to the right, and placed in between the first and second corrugations from the ISO post. The KS Line logos have been painted out after Hanjin took over KS Line containers. Photographed in October 1989.

KSCU 414406 is another 40 bevel corrugated side container. Series is 413000-414899 (1,900 containers). The table below shows the weights and measures data from this container. Photographed on March 27, 1986.

MAX. GROSS	30480	KGS
	67200	LBS
TARE	3660	KGS
	8069	LBS
NET.	26820	KGS
	59131	LBS
CU.CAP.	67.4	M³
	2380	FT³

Roster of Hanjin Container Lines								
Marks	Number Range		OL	OH	OW	Quantity	Type	Notes
HJCU	690001	690300	40	9-6	8	300	Refrigerated	
HJCU	700000	702899	40	8-6	8	2900	Dry Van	
HJCU	702900	703699	40	8-6	8	800	Dry Van	
HJCU	703700	703899	40	8-6	8	200	Dry Van	
HJCU	703900	703909	40	8-6	8	10	Dry Van	
HJCU	704001	704900	40	8-6	8	900	Dry Van	
HJCU	704901	705100	40	8-6	8	200	Dry Van	
HJCU	705101	705400	40	8-6	8	300	Dry Van	
HJCU	705401	705600	40	8-6	8	200	Dry Van	
HJCU	705601	705700	40	8-6	8	100	Dry Van	
HJCU	705701	705800	40	8-6	8	100	Dry Van	
HJCU	705801	706100	40	8-6	8	300	Dry Van	
HJCU	706101	706350	40	8-6	8	250	Dry Van	
HJCU	706351	706700	40	8-6	8	350	Dry Van	
HJCU	706701	707000	40	8-6	8	300	Dry Van	
HJCU	707001	707300	40	8-6	8	300	Dry Van	
HJCU	707301	708300	40	8-6	8	1000	Dry Van	
HJCU	708301	708800	40	8-6	8	500	Dry Van	
HJCU	708801	709300	40	8-6	8	500	Dry Van	
HJCU	709301	711800	40	8-6	8	2500	Dry Van	
HJCU	711801	715300	40	8-6	8	3500	Dry Van	
HJCU	715301	715500	40	8-6	8	200	Dry Van	
HJCU	715501	715800	40	8-6	8	300	Dry Van	
HJCU	715801	717800	40	8-6	8	2000	Dry Van	
HJCU	717801	721600	40	8-6	8	3800	Dry Van	
HJCU	770001	770500	40	9-6	8	500	Dry Van	
HJCU	770501	772500	40	9-6	8	2000	Dry Van	
HJCU	772501	772650	40	9-6	8	150	Dry Van	
HJCU	772651	772800	40	9-6	8	150	Dry Van	
HJCU	772801	773500	40	9-6	8	700	Dry Van	
HJCU	773501	774500	40	9-6	8	1000	Dry Van	
HJCU	774501	774800	40	9-6	8	300	Dry Van	
HJCU	774801	775800	40	9-6	8	1000	Dry Van	
HJCU	775801	776800	40	9-6	8	1000	Dry Van	
HJCU	820001	820200	20	8-6	8	200	Dry Van	
HJCU	850001	851800	20	8-6	8	1800	Dry Van	
HJCU	851801	853307	20	8-6	8	1507	Dry Van	
KSCU	211000	211579	20	8-6	8	580	Dry Van	

Roster of Hanjin Container Lines								
Marks	Number Range		OL	OH	OW	Quantity	Type	Notes
KSCU	212000	212749	20	8-6	8	750	Dry Van	
KSCU	213000	214399	20	8-6	8	1400	Dry Van	
KSCU	215000	216699	20	8-6	8	1700	Dry Van	
KSCU	411000	411979	40	8-6	8	980	Dry Van	
KSCU	412000	412699	40	8-6	8	700	Dry Van	
KSCU	413000	414899	40	8-6	8	1900	Dry Van	
KSCU	415000	416399	40	8-6	8	1400	Dry Van	

Table includes containers coming on line from Korea Shipping Line circa 1987-88.

HJCU 715957. Standard-height 40-foot dry van container. The more modern three-pin vents can be seen on this container.

Field Notes
HJCU 700759. Built 1-79 by Hyundai. Type HD-1AA-250. Construction No. HDHJ79-400760.

HJCU 709763. Built 5-86 by Hyundai. Type HD-1AA-256. Construction No. HDHJ86-404262.

HJCU 850447. Built 5-85 by HMIC. Type HC-1319.

KSCU 413547, Built 9-85 by Hyundai. Type HD-1AA-815. This container also carries an XTRA identification, XTRU 412364.

CTI — Container Transport International

A decades old company in the container leasing business by the time the Eighties rolled around, CTI had a fleet of over 300,000 containers by the mid-Eighties.

In the 1980s, CTI's container fleet was made up of mostly 20-foot containers (19'11"). In fact, 20-foot containers outnumbered 40-foot containers by nearly 3 to 1.

CTIU 324093 is typical of the huge fleet of 20-foot containers owned by CTI. Square side and front wall corrugations, two logo panels with removable vent covers, and flat doors with "OTI" handles. This sits on chassis TAXZ 224464. The table to the right shows the weights and capacities as shown on the container. Hanover, PA. *John L. Becker photo.*

MGW.	20,320	KG
	44,800	LBS
TARE.	2,300	KG
	5,070	LBS
NET.	18,020	KG
	39,730	LBS
CU.CAP.	33.0	CU.MT.
	1,165	CU.FT.

CTIU 020417. Decades before the current trend to use numbers with leading zeros, CTI was using them back in the Seventies. This container is a 19'11" standard-height dry van container. The vent casings across the top of each logo panel have had repairs made, usually to clean out the openings. There are four fork lift pockets; two for loaded and two for empty. Sides are square corrugated in a 2-17-2 arrangement. Photographed on January 11, 1986 in Los Angeles, CA

CTIU 026968, the inspiration for digital camouflage (okay, probably not). But, judging by the paint patches around the vent covers, the originals have been replaced with the eight-pin plastic removable covers. Side rails on both this and the previous container are a stepped design. Chassis is TLCC 00268-63 built by Gindy.

CTIU 048005 is a 19'11" standard-height dry van container. The design differs a bit from the previous two containers. The front ISO posts are stepped between it and the first corrugation, making it appear similar to the grooved ISO posts on early Hanjin containers. The rear ISO post is solid. Flanged lower side rails.

CTIU 082143. This is a 19'11" standard-height dry van container. This one has a solid lower slide rail. Again, the container morphologist is challenged by ISO post and corrugation design. The corrugations adjacent to the ISO posts do not have a full "valley" separating the two features. Vent covers are steel, not an easily removable design. Photographed at the Southern Pacific City of Industry yard during the early 1980s.

CTIU 111996. Standard-height 20-foot dry van container. Leased to Contship as indicated by the vertical logo on the right side. The table to the right gives the weights and capacities as shown on the actual container. Kingsport, TN. *John L. Becker photo.*

MGW.	20,320	KG
	44,800	LBS
TARE.	2,350	KG
	5,204	LBS
NET.	17,960	KG
	39,596	LBS
CU.CAP.	32.8	CU.MT.
	1,158	CU.FT.

Field Notes
CTIU 433863. US 4310. Built 3-80 by Alna Koki. Type ADS6A.

CTIU 434421. Built 5-78 by Tokyu Car. Type DAA-136BS.

CTIU 443799. US 4310. Built 12-78 by Pusan Steel, Korea. Type PS-CT-7846.

CTIU 451738. Built 6-80 by Sharyo. Type AA1211A-1.

CTIU 458414. Built 6-80 by Alna Koki.

CTIU 487504. US 4310. Built 10-80 by Korea Container Industrial Co. Ltd. Busan Factory. Type KC40-502 B(L). 2373 cf.

CTIU 523178, US 4310. Built 8-86 by Hyundai. Type HD-1AA-304. Tare 8,400 lbs. 2387 cf.

CTIU 115112 straight-on front view showing the eight squared corrugated front wall. There are three panels clearly seen by the weld lines arranged in a 2-4-2 configuration. Photographed in December 1989.

CTIU 121858. Standard-height 19'11" dry van container. Flanged lower side rail. Square corrugated 2-17-2 side. Vent casings located in the upper part of the logo panels are a steel, fixed type. IC 87. ISO size-type code is 2210. Photographed in the early 1980s in Mojave, CA.

CTIU 124545. Standard-height 19'11" dry van container. Flanged lower side rail. Square corrugated 2-17-2 side. Vent casings located in the upper part of the logo panels are a steel, not easily removable type. Placards, paint patches and repairs are typical in-service views of containers of container leasing companies after years of service in the trade. The railcar is a Trailer Train class RSF50 spine car built by Trinity Industries in 5-87. Photographed in November 1989.

CTIU 129101. Standard-height 19'11" dry van container. Square corrugated 2-17-2 side. Vent casings located in the upper part of the logo panels are a steel, fixed type. Stepped lower side rail. Eight square corrugated front wall. Photographed in December 1989.

CTIU 147189 has lost one of its vents on this side (to the right). Interesting patch repairs. You can see weld seams where the physical repairs were made, followed by the patch of fresh paint. Chassis is a Strick-built Barber Lines' BBSZ 220841. Hanover, PA. *John L. Becker photo.*

CTIU 167137 is backed up against the docks. This one has the flanged lower side rail. Eight corrugation front wall. Eight-pin plastic removable vent covers centered at the top of each logo panel. Hanover, PA. *John L.Becker photo.*

CTIU 184312. The vent cover on the left in this photo is original. The other vent cover is a replacement, one of the eight-pin plastic removable types. Standard-height 19'11" dry van container. Stepped lower side rail. Square corrugated 2-17-2 side. Photographed in December 1989.

CTIU 227571. The vent covers on this one bridges the entire top of each logo panel. Flat doors. "OTI" handles. The sides are 2-17-2 square corrugated. Stepped lower side rail. The table to the right shows the text of the weights and capacities data on the right door. This one was being leased to Farrell Lines.

MGW.	20,320	KG
	44,800	LBS
TARE.	2,330	KG
	5,140	LBS
NET.	17,990	KG
	39,660	LBS
CU.CAP.	33.0	CU.MT.
	1,165	CU.FT.

CTIU 252339 side view with square corrugated 2-17-2 sides and vents the same as CTIU 227571.

CTIU 252339 roster view showing the flat doors and "OTI" handles. The Bureau Veritas certification label can be seen in the upper left hand corner of the left door.

CTIU 300867. Another 2-17-2 side configuration. Flanged lower side rail. Although it's barely visible, this container is being moved on one of Santa Fe's bulkhead flat cars (the bulkhead can be seen to the right). During the initial ramp up of container loadings in the mid-Eighties, the Santa Fe employed many types of flat and even gondola cars. December 14, 1985.

CTIU 306120. Standard-height 19'11" dry van container. This one was leased to APL at one time (note the APL sticker above the 2.6 label in the lower right logo panel). Chassis is a Uni-*Flex* UFCC 4882. Photographed on January 19, 1986 in the Port of LA/Long Beach area.

CTIU 310698. A nice shiny, new 19'11" standard-height dry van container. Note the fresh sealant around the vent housings. Chassis is a Uni-*Flex* UFCC 40324. Photographed at Kruse in El Monte California in March 1981.

CTIU 314580. And only eight years later, a container from the same group as CTIU 310698 shows its wear. The table below gives CTIU 314580's weights and capacities as shown on the container.

MGW.	20,320	KG
	44,800	LBS
TARE.	2,300	KG
	5,070	LBS
NET.	18,020	KG
	39,730	LBS
CU.CAP.	33.0	CU.MT.
	1,165	CU.FT.

(Right). CTIU 320362 direct front view clearly shows two panels of four corrugations each. Also, the container ID is placed vertically between the first and second corrugation from the right. Compare to the front view of CTIU 115112.

The chassis is FLXZ 12349 and was assigned to APL at one time as indicated by the chalk marks. December 1989.

CTIU 328366. The vent casings on these are the eight-pin plastic easily-removable style located at the top of each logo panel. Having removable vent casings allows quick access to clean out the vent holes. Photographed on September 21, 1985.

CTIU 328433 was built in October 1982. Builder and type — Civet SC-20-2. Flanged lower side rail is evident in this photo. Chassis is Nautilus owned HCLZ 200324. May 26, 1983

CTIU 345359 direct view of front. The front wall on this one is made up of two panels of four corrugations each. The unit ID is horizontal offset near the top of the front wall. The chassis is FLXZ 10664 and was at one time leased to APL as indicated by the red and white sticker on the left side. Photographed in December 1989.

CTIU 425331. Standard-height 40-foot dry van container. This container has a total of 48 corrugations made up of ten panels in a 3L1-5-5-5-5-5-5-5-5-1L3 configuration. Flat doors with handles "OTI" style. Stepped lower side rail. Vent casings permanent and fill the top area of the logo panels. Photographed in December 1989.

CTIU 438568 direct view of the doors showing the markings layout and physical features. Flat doors. "OTI" handles. Bureau Veritas certification label is above the "c" in "cti". There is a small yellow and blue "On Lease To Farrell Lines" label to the right of the top handle on the right door. The table below gives the weights and capacities as displayed on the container.

MGW.	30,480	KG
	67,200	LBS
TARE.	4,060	KG
	8,950	LBS
NET.	26,420	KG
	58,250	LBS
CU.CAP.	66.3	CU.MT.
	2,341	CU.FT.

CTIU 438568. This container has a total of 46 corrugations arranged in a 2-42-2 configuration. While this container is marked as an ISO size-type code 4310 (vented 40-foot standard-height dry van), the vents, at least on this side, have been removed. Chassis is APL operated APLZ 133543. Photographed in December 1989.

CTIU 448748 is another 46 corrugation container. This one has the vent casings located on the top of the logo panels. Weights and capacities are the same as the previous container, CTIU 438568, except the CU.MT./CU.FT. is 66.9/2363.

Number Range		OL	OH	OW	Quantity	Type
	Condensed Roster[1] of CTIU containers during the 1980s[2]					
010001	012595	19-11	8-6	8	2,595	Dry Van
012601	017100	19-11	8-6	8	4,500	Dry Van
017601	028490	19-11	8-6	8	10,890	Dry Van
028501	033820	19-11	8-6	8	5,320	Dry Van
033901	038090	19-11	8-6	8	4,190	Dry Van
038101	046870	19-11	8-6	8	8,770	Dry Van
046901	059800	19-11	8-6	8	12,900	Dry Van
060001	061205	19-11	8-6	8	1,205	Dry Van
061206	061275	19-11	8	8	70	Dry Van
061301	062801	19-11	8	8	1,501	Dry Van
063036	063275	19-11	8	8	240	Dry Van
063296	063675	19-11	8-6	8	380	Dry Van
063676	064175	19-11	8	8	500	Dry Van
064276	064375	19-11	8	8	100	Dry Van
064426	065895	19-11	8	8	1,470	Dry Van
065976	066241	19-11	8	8	266	Dry Van
066276	066499	19-11	8	8	224	Dry Van
066593	068648	19-11	8	8	2,056	Dry Van
068700	069499	19-11	8	8	800	Dry Van
070001	070400	19-11	8-6	8	400	Dry Van
070600	073536	19-11	8	8	2,937	Dry Van
074001	074860	19-11	8	8	860	Dry Van
075001	075144	19-11	8	8	144	Dry Van
078401	078700	19-11	8	8	300	Dry Van
080001	080370	19-11	8-6	8	370	Dry Van
082001	083400	19-11	8-6	8	1,400	Dry Van
083501	089950	19-11	8-6	8	6,450	Dry Van
090001	091000	40	8-6	8	1,000	Dry Van
099105	099999	19-11	8-6	8	895	Dry Van
100001	102900	19-11	8-6	8	2,900	Dry Van
103101	106700	19-11	8-6	8	3,600	Dry Van
106851	107800	19-11	8-6	8	950	Dry Van
108301	110925	19-11	8-6	8	2,625	Dry Van
111001	112999	19-11	8-6	8	1,999	Dry Van
113001	118175	19-11	8-6	8	5,175	Dry Van
118276	133350	19-11	8-6	8	15,075	Dry Van
134000	134849	19-11	8-6	8	850	Dry Van
134950	140489	19-11	8-6	8	5,540	Dry Van
142000	149594	19-11	8-6	8	7,595	Dry Van
150000	153624	19-11	8-6	8	3,625	Dry Van
154000	170399	19-11	8-6	8	16,400	Dry Van

(Left) CTIU 452978 showing the interior of the container in the door area. Note the 27 holes, which perform the ventilation by allowing air in from outside the container. A single lashing ring can be seen directly above the unit ID. Containers are usually equipped with a variable quantity of lashing rings. These help secure the load better. Light gray painted interiors are common. Photographed in November 1989.

(Below) CTIU 452978. Standard-height 40-foot dry van container. The vents on this container are the eight-pin plastic removable type. Chassis is FLXZ 41020 assigned to Neptune Orient Lines. Tare weight of the chassis is 6,750 lbs. Photographed in November 1989.

\multicolumn{6}{c}{Condensed Roster[1] of CTIU containers during the 1980s[2]}
Number Range		OL	OH	OW	Quantity	Type
---	---	---	---	---	---	---
170626	177399	19-11	8-6	8	6,774	Dry Van
178000	181364	19-11	8-6	8	3,365	Dry Van
182000	191239	19-11	8-6	8	9,240	Dry Van
193000	193515	19-11	8-6	8	516	Dry Van
194000	194670	19-11	8-6	8	671	Dry Van
195000	195143	19-11	8-6	8	144	Dry Van
196000	197094	19-11	8-6	8	1,095	Dry Van
200000	200000	19-11	8-6	8	1	Dry Van
200676	200775	40	8-6	8	100	Dry Van
200876	200974	40	8-6	8	99	Dry Van
201070	201169	40	8-6	8	100	Dry Van
202001	202099	40	8-6	8	99	Dry Van
206000	206199	40	8-6	8	200	Dry Van
206600	206849	40	8-6	8	250	Dry Van
206850	206949	40	8-6	8	100	Dry Van
206950	207499	40	8-6	8	550	Dry Van
207500	207599	40	8-6	8	100	Dry Van
207602	207801	40	8-6	8	200	Dry Van
207802	207901	40	8-6	8	100	Dry Van
207902	208196	40	8-6	8	295	Dry Van
208227	208326	40	8-6	8	100	Dry Van
208327	208716	40	8-6	8	390	Dry Van
210208	210233	19-11	8	8	26	Dry Van
215301	215700	40	8-6	8	400	Dry Van
220001	240000	19-11	8-6	8	20,000	Dry Van
240066	240693	19-11	8-6	8	628	Dry Van
240700	240918	19-11	8-6	8	219	Dry Van
241000	259975	19-11	8-6	8	18,976	Dry Van
260001	260384	19-11	8	8	384	Dry Van
260553	260776	19-11	8	8	224	Dry Van
261001	261300	19-11	8	8	300	Dry Van
261301	261350	19-11	8	8	50	Dry Van
261501	262000	19-11	8	8	500	Dry Van
262100	262249	19-11	8	8	150	Dry Van
262300	262549	19-11	8	8	250	Dry Van
262650	262749	19-11	8	8	100	Dry Van
263000	263399	19-11	8	8	400	Dry Van
263500	263999	19-11	8	8	500	Dry Van
264100	264155	19-11	8	8	56	Dry Van
264415	264814	19-11	8	8	400	Dry Van
264815	264895	19-11	8	8	81	Dry Van

Condensed Roster[1] of CTIU containers during the 1980s[2]

Number Range		OL	OH	OW	Quantity	Type
264896	267999	19-11	8	8	3,104	Dry Van
268001	268100	19-11	8	8	100	Dry Van
268280	268379	19-11	8	8	100	Dry Van
268400	269449	19-11	8	8	1,050	Dry Van
269499	269999	19-11	8	8	501	Dry Van
270000	270199	19-11	8	8	200	Dry Van
270200	271199	19-11	8	8	1,000	Dry Van
271399	272698	19-11	8	8	1,300	Dry Van
272799	272978	19-11	8	8	180	Dry Van
272999	273725	19-11	8	8	727	Dry Van
273901	274876	19-11	8	8	976	Dry Van
275001	277675	19-11	8	8	2,675	Dry Van
277826	277945	19-11	8	8	120	Dry Van
278242	278301	19-11	8	8	60	Dry Van
278326	278750	19-11	8	8	425	Dry Van
278826	279105	19-11	8	8	280	Dry Van
279226	279319	19-11	8	8	94	Dry Van
279326	279726	19-11	8	8	401	Dry Van
279750	279799	19-11	8	8	50	Dry Van
280000	289999	19-11	8-6	8	10,000	Dry Van
290001	294403	40	8-6	8	4,403	Dry Van
294501	297340	40	8-6	8	2,840	Dry Van
297401	299855	40	8-6	8	2,455	Dry Van
299870	299970	40	8-6	8	101	Dry Van
300000	315850	19-11	8-6	8	15,851	Dry Van
320000	329999	19-11	8-6	8	10,000	Dry Van
330000	330281	19-11	8-6	8	282	Dry Van
331100	331994	19-11	8-6	8	895	Dry Van
340000	343669	19-11	8-6	8	3,670	Dry Van
343670	346484	19-11	8	8	2,815	Dry Van
359901	360000	19-11	8	8	100	Flat Rack
360186	360348	19-11	8	8	163	Flat Rack
401000	401049	40	8-6	8	50	Dry Van
401100	401889	40	8-6	8	790	Dry Van
402000	403744	40	8-6	8	1,745	Dry Van
404045	404484	40	8-6	8	440	Dry Van
411001	417700	40	8-6	8	6,700	Dry Van
417901	418098	40	8-6	8	198	Dry Van
418101	437995	40	8-6	8	19,895	Dry Van
438001	457874	40	8-6	8	19,874	Dry Van
458000	459999	40	8-6	8	2,000	Dry Van

Condensed Roster[1] of CTIU containers during the 1980s[2]						
Number Range		OL	OH	OW	Quantity	Type
460031	460080	19-11	8	8	50	Open Top
460151	460215	19-11	8	8	65	Open Top
460216	460263	19-11	8	8	48	Open Top
460364	460381	19-11	8	8	18	Open Top
460382	460481	19-11	8	8	100	Open Top
460482	460581	19-11	8	8	100	Open Top
460597	460616	19-11	8	8	20	Open Top
460727	460876	19-11	8-6	8	150	Dry Van
461001	461100	19-11	8	8	100	Dry Van
470001	470200	40	8-6	8	200	Dry Van
480000	481999	40	8-6	8	2,000	Dry Van
482000	484974	40	8-6	8	2,975	Dry Van
485000	496954	40	8-6	8	11,955	Dry Van
497000	497959	40	8-6	8	960	Dry Van
498000	498354	40	8-6	8	355	Dry Van
499000	499900	40	8-6	8	901	Dry Van
500311	500322	40	8-6	8	12	Refrigerated
510000	510019	19-11	8-6	8	20	Refrigerated
520000	520639	40	8-6	8	640	Dry Van
521000	523777	40	8-6	8	2,778	Dry Van
530000	533056	40	8-6	8	3,057	Dry Van
534000	534764	40	8-6	8	765	Dry Van
560000	561499	40	8-6	8	1,500	Dry Van
600000	600219	19-11	8-6	8	220	Flat Rack
960010	960809	40	9-6	8	800	Dry Van

[1] Does not represent specific orders or builders. Series have been combined based on size and type.

[2] Does not include containers in closed interchange outside of the United States and Canada.

CTIU 494661. Standard-height 40-foot dry van container. Vent casings centered at the top of each logo panel. Flat doors with OTI handles. The flat car is TTWX 922250 built by ACF in February 1980. Trailer Train class ASH22. Photographed on October 2, 1985.

CTIU 960741. High-cube 40-foot dry van container. CTI only fielded one group of 800 high-cube 40-foot containers at this time. Series, CTIU 960010-960809. Also uncommon is the large "billboard" style lessee's letter-logo on the side, in this case Barber Blue Sea. Barber Blue Sea shipping was a joint venture between Blue Funnel and the Norwegian firms Wilhelmsen and Brostrøms. Photographed in October 1981.

United States Lines Containers

United States Lines was originally formed in 1921, operating passenger service until 1969. Containerization trailblazer Malcolm McClean acquired U.S. Lines in 1978 and expanded its container services. U.S. Lines filed for bankruptcy in 1986. Cargo service lasted until 1987 (with reduced service to 1989).

USLU 100943. One of 44,600 steel corrugated standard-height 40-foot containers delivered U.S. Lines during the mid-1980s. The design featured beveled 2-35-2 sides with eight-pin plastic vent casings centered in the upper logo panels. The doors have 1-3-1 squared corrugations with "OTI" handles (**O**utside handles are on **T**op facing **I**nside). The front wall has eight corrugations.

Partial Roster of USLU containers 1980-1985							
Number Range		OL	OH	OW	Type	Quantity	Notes
100000	144599	40	8-6	8	Dry Van	44,600	S
200001	200600	19-11	8	8	Dry Van	600	Fa
200601	202300	19-11	8	8	Dry Van	1,700	A
202301	203500	19-11	8	8	Dry Van	1,200	A
203551	203851	19-11	8	8	Dry Van	301	A
208001	208400	19-11	8	8	Dry Van	400	A
209001	209151	19-11	8	8	Dry Van	151	A
210000	210999	19-10	8-6	8	Dry Van	1,000	Fs
211000	211999	19-10	8-6	8	Dry Van	1,000	Fs
212000	212999	19-10	8-6	8	Dry Van	1,000	Fs
300000	300049	40	8-6	8	Refrigerated	50	2
400001	400175	40	8	8	Dry Van	175	A
400176	401985	40	8	8	Dry Van	1,810	A
402001	402300	40	8-6	8	Dry Van	300	A
409001	409025	40	8	8	Dry Van	25	A, C
409031	409530	40	8-6	8	Dry Van	500	A
410001	410955	40	8-6	8	Dry Van	955	A
410956	411255	40	8-6	8	Dry Van	300	A
411256	413255	40	8-6	8	Dry Van	2,000	A
413256	413317	40	8-6	8	Dry Van	62	A
413318	413345	40	8-6	8	Dry Van	28	A
413356	417355	40	8-6	8	Dry Van	4,000	A
417356	418105	40	8-6	8	Dry Van	750	A
418581	418740	40	8-6	8	Dry Van	160	A
418800	418820	40	8-6	8	Dry Van	21	A
418850	419939	40	8-6	8	Dry Van	1,090	A
420016	420615	40	8-6	8	Dry Van	600	A
420616	420999	40	8-6	8	Dry Van	384	A
421000	421999	40	8-6	8	Dry Van	1,000	A
422001	422116	40	8-6	8	Dry Van	116	A
422117	425716	40	8-6	8	Dry Van	3,600	A
425717	428716	40	8-6	8	Dry Van	3,000	A
430001	430475	40	8-6	8	Refrigerated	475	2
430476	430620	40	8-6	8	Refrigerated	145	1
430621	430820	40	8-6	8	Refrigerated	200	3
430821	430920	40	8-6	8	Refrigerated	100	3
431000	431011	40	8-6	8	Refrigerated	12	3
431012	431063	40	8-6	8	Refrigerated	52	2

Partial Roster of USLU containers 1980-1985							
Number Range		OL	OH	OW	Type	Quantity	Notes
431064	431215	40	8-6	8	Refrigerated	152	2
434501	434550	40	8-6	8	Refrigerated	50	2
434552	434601	40	8-6	8	Refrigerated	50	1
438000	438149	40	8-6	8	Refrigerated	150	1
439001	439010	40	8-6	8	Refrigerated	10	2
439011	439062	40	8-6	8	Refrigerated	52	4
440001	440045	40	4-3	8	Open-Top	45	
451001	451165	40	8-6	8	Open-Top	165	A
451166	451365	40	8-6	8	Open-Top	200	Fs
460000	460749	40	8-6	8	Dry Van	750	S
460750	461499	40	8-6	8	Dry Van	750	S
480001	480100	40	4-3	8	Tank	100	T
496001	496700	40	9-6	8	Dry Van	700	A
497173	497178	40	8	8-1	Flat Rack	6	

Notes

Non-Refrigerated:
Note A. Steel-framed aluminum body.
Note C. Equipped with a curbside door.
Note Fa. Aluminum-framed FRP body.
Note Fs. Steel-framed FRP body.
Note S. Steel-framed, steel body
Note T. Capacity 6,020 gallons.

Refrigerated:
Note 1. Carrier refrigeration with diesel generator.
Note 2. Thermo-King refrigeration with diesel generator.
Note 3. Refrigeration unit with diesel generator.
Note 4. Refrigeration unit amd polar stream nitrogen system.

USLU 101724 has already had one vent casing replaced with a four-pin casing (left vent). Chassis is USLZ 926024.

USLU 113044 on chassis USLU 973461 (U.S. Lines was converting to "Z" for chassis, but many remained ending in "U"). Flat car is TTX 160034 built in March 1974 and repaired and repainted in May 1983 by Cal Pro, Mira Loma, CA.

USLU 113342 and USLU 142625 at the City of Industry, CA in February 1986.

USLU 136590 on Trailer Train flat TTWX 972127 built in September 1968. Photographed on March 27, 1986.

USLU 114654 and USLU 101719 on Trailer Train's TTWX 973038 (built 3-73).
Photographed in February 1986.

USLU 119031 on Trailer Train's TTWX 990317 (built 9-79, PS).

USLU 120666 on one of the relatively few Trailer Train 89'4" intermodal flats equipped for containers only at delivery. TTCX 975088 was built in October 1968. Photographed on January 26, 1986.

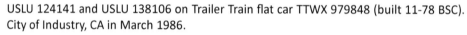

USLU 124141 and USLU 138106 on Trailer Train flat car TTWX 979848 (built 11-78 BSC). City of Industry, CA in March 1986.

USLU 124652 on chassis USLZ 926082. Flat car is ATSF 297047.

USLU 125217 on a Trailer Train class PSH10A intermodal flat car. Photographed on March 27, 1986.

USLU 129345 shows off its roof with 22 widely spaced corrugations. The flat is MP 838285 converted by FWRS in 5-79. Photographed on May 17, 1986.

USLU 132104. The flat car, SP 901708 was converted at the Southern Pacific Shops in March 1985.

USLU 132104 side view. The 85' flat car is SP 901708. It was rebuilt in 3-85 at the Southern Pacific Shops.

USLU 133145. Trailer Train flat car TTWX 991399 was built in 10-79 by Pullman-Standard.

USLU 135608. The 85' flat car is an SP 901636 built in 11-62 according to the COTS. It was rebuilt as part of a program to convert applicable flat cars into intermodal cars. This one was rebuilt by the Pine Bluffs Shop in 1-85. SP class F-70-48 R. Equipped with Keystone 10" cushioning. Light weight, 67,500 lbs.

USLU 140500 on Interpool owned, Strick-built chassis IRSZ 178859. May 24, 1986

USLU 210516 (above) and USLU 210547 (below). Series 210000-210999 (1,000 units). Both built by Theurer. Max Gross 44,800 lbs 20,321 kgs. Tare Weight 4,350 lbs 1,973 kgs. Max Cargo 40,450 lbs 18,348 kgs. Cubic Capacity 1,187.6 cu.ft. 33.6 cu.m. These are 19'10" OL x 8'6" OH x 8' OW steel-framed FRP sides containers. February 1986. City of Industry, CA.

USLU 212244 is another steel-framed FRP sides 20' container. Series is 212000-212999 (1,000 units). The Theurer builder's logo is located toward the front on both sides. Photographed on March 27, 1986.

USLU 411988 is a 19 exterior-post side 40-foot standard-height container. Chassis USLU 946037. May 24, 1986.

USLU 413845. Steel-framed 40-foot standard-height aluminum sheet-and-post container. The sides have nine-full-width panels plus the narrow panels at each end. Chassis is USLZ 925947.

USLU 414715. Note the four hinge doors with a plate connecting lower and upper hinges into pairs. Steel-framed 40-foot standard-height aluminum sheet-and-post container. Max. Gross 30,480 kgs 67,200 lbs. Tare Wgt. 2,767 kgs 6,100 lbs. Max Cargo 27,715 kgs 61,100 lbs. Flat car MEC 105114 (PS Lot 1016).

USLU 419908. Eight full-width panels plus narrower end panels. Three (six-pin) hinged doors with ITO handles (**I**nside handles are on **T**op facing **O**utward). Built by Mitsubishi. Note the container's identification marks are centered on the sides above the logo near the roof line. Flat car is VTTX 301876.

USLU 422486. Nine full-width panel aluminum sheet-and-post design. Now the ISO Type Code appears on all sides (4300). The doors have four hinges (each with four pins). Series is USLU 422117-425716 (2,200 units).

USLU 423910. Here we can see the four exterior-post front wall of the 422117-425716 series. Also, this series sports a new side logo, a three line red and blue "United States Lines" in a white box. Side container identification marks, country code and ISO type code are always to the right, but the logo is always toward the front on this series. Flat car is TTCX 975165.

USLU 424728. Again note the USL boxed logo is toward the front. Built by Nippon Fruehauf in 1980. Model KADX 40 TJ. Flat car is TTLX 500757.

USLU 427419 has ten full-width panel sides on this aluminum sheet-and-post design. The doors each have three four-pin hinges. This container features yet another paint scheme for the 40-foot standard-heights, with the single line "United States Lines" under the USL seal. Photographed on December 23, 1985.

USLU 496192, the only series of dry van high-cube 40-foot containers. Note the ISO Type Code "4000" which at the time was the "other" height category for 40-footers. Aluminum, sheet-and-post construction. Series 496001-496700 (700 units). There is a red warning label identifying this container as a 9'6" hight container. Note also the small blue round ABS logo in the corner.

CPSIA information can be obtained
at www.ICGtesting.com
Printed in the USA
BVHW020416151121
621673BV00006B/481